JOHANN SEBASTIAN BACH

KONZERT

d-Moll / D minor

für Cembalo (Klavier) und Streicher
for Harpsichord (Piano) and Strings

BWV 1052

Nach den Quellen herausgegeben von / Edited from the sources by
Hans-Joachim Schulze

Ausgabe für zwei Klaviere von / Edition for two Pianos by
Klaus Schubert

EIGENTUM DES VERLEGERS · ALLE RECHTE VORBEHALTEN
ALL RIGHTS RESERVED

C. F. PETERS

FRANKFURT/M. · LEIPZIG · LONDON · NEW YORK

I. Allegro 3

II. Adagio 31

III. Allegro 38

Vorliegende Ausgabe basiert auf der Urtext-Partiturausgabe EP 9384
The present edition is based on the urtext edition of the full score EP 9384

Aufführungsmaterial käuflich erhältlich / Orchestral material available for sale

Aufführungsdauer / Duration: ca. 24 Min.

KONZERT

d-Moll / D minor

für Cembalo (Klavier) und Streicher

Johann Sebastian Bach (1685-1750)
BWV 1052
Herausgegeben von Hans-Joachim Schulze

Klavier I
Cembalo concertato

Klavier II
(Streichorchester)

16

20

52

Nachwort

Johann Sebastian Bachs Cembalokonzerte BWV 1052-1058 gelten heute ohne Ausnahme als Bearbeitungen älterer, größerenteils verlorengegangener Werke, die als Soloinstrument hauptsächlich die Violine verwendeten. Über den Anlaß zur Übertragung auf das Tasteninstrument ist nichts überliefert; da die Merkmale der glücklicherweise erhaltengebliebenen autographen Partitur (Deutsche Staatsbibliothek zu Berlin, *Mus. ms. autogr. Bach P 234*, Sammelhandschrift mit sieben Cembalokonzerten) jedoch auf die zweite Hälfte der 1730er Jahre deuten, wird man auf einen Zusammenhang mit dem „Bachischen Collegium Musicum" schließen dürfen, dessen Leitung der Thomaskantor nach fast zweijähriger Unterbrechung im September 1739 wieder übernommen hatte. Über die Art der Darbietung (Bach selbst oder einer seiner Söhne und Schüler als Solisten) und über die Aufnahme durch die Zeitgenossen ist man auf Vermutungen angewiesen; es scheint aber, daß das d-Moll-Konzert BWV 1052 schon bald eine gewisse Vorzugsstellung eingenommen hat.

Dies ist allein schon an Zahl und Qualität erhaltener Abschriften zu erkennen. Wiederaufführungen um und nach 1750 in Berlin sind als in hohem Grade wahrscheinlich anzusehen, und in einem Frühstadium der Bach-Pflege des 19. Jahrhunderts läßt sich wiederum eine Darbietung nachweisen, die 1807 in der Berliner Singakademie stattfand. Die Weiterführung dieser Tradition lag in den Händen von Felix Mendelssohn Bartholdy, der das Konzert seit spätestens 1835 in seinem Repertoire führte. Mendelssohns Leipziger Gewandhausaufführung vom 9. März 1837 dürfte den Anstoß gegeben haben, das von Robert Schumann als „hochberühmt" bezeichnete Konzert als erstes Bachsches Orchesterwerk überhaupt im Druck herauszugeben. Der Erstveröffentlichung der Partitur im Verlag Friedrich Kistner (Leipzig 1838) folgten Neudrucke auf breiterer Quellenbasis: 1854 bei C. F. Peters und 1869 in Band 17 der Gesamtausgabe der Bach-Gesellschaft.

Gleichwohl hat die Bach-Forschung seit längerem Zweifel an der Echtheit des Werkes gehegt, die auch durch den schon früh erfolgten Hinweis auf ein verschollenes Violinkonzert als Grundlage der Bachschen Cembalotranskription nicht ausgeräumt werden konnten. Nicht zu trennen ist diese Echtheitsfrage von der verwickelten Entstehungsgeschichte des Werkes in seinen verschiedenen Fassungen, die sich nach heutiger Kenntnis wie folgt darstellt: Alle erhaltenen Gestalten scheinen zurückzugehen auf ein Violinkonzert in d-Moll, das zwar nicht erhaltengeblieben ist, sich jedoch hinreichend zuverlässig rekonstruieren läßt. Ob die Thematik, die Violintechnik und die ungleichwertige kontrapunktische Verarbeitung es erlauben, dieses erschlossene Konzert in allen Teilen als Schöpfung J. S. Bachs anzusehen, muß dahingestellt bleiben. Als Entstehungszeit kommen die letzten Weimarer Jahre Bachs (1714-1717) wohl eher in Frage als die anschließende Köthener Meisterzeit.

Die frühesten Spuren einer Umarbeitung des Violinkonzertes liegen in zwei Kirchenkantaten vor, von denen die Kantate 146 lediglich eine hypothetische Datierung zuläßt, während die Entstehung der Kantate 188 ziemlich sicher 1729 angenommen werden kann. Beide Kantaten verwenden als Einleitung je einen der schnellen Sätze unseres Konzertes, besetzt mit Orgel, Streichern und Holzbläsern, Kantate 146 präsentiert zudem den langsamen Satz in kühner Umgestaltung zum vierstimmigen Chor; so liegt es nahe, beide Kantaten in zeitlicher Nachbarschaft anzusetzen. Etwa 1732/34 schrieb Carl Philipp Emanuel Bach eine Transkription für Cembalo und Streicher (BWV 1052a) in Stimmen nieder, möglicherweise für den Vortrag im Collegium Musicum seines Vaters bestimmt.

Gegen Ende der 1730er Jahre nahm Johann Sebastian Bach, wie bereits angedeutet, selbst eine Umarbeitung vor. Während die Streicherstimmen nur geringfügige Retuschen erfuhren, veränderte Bach die als Cembalodiskant eingetragene Soloviolinstimme sowie die für den Cembalobaß weitgehend herangezogene Lesart der Continuostimme in vielfältiger Weise, um den Solopart dem Charakter des Tasteninstruments stärker anzupassen. Bei der Ausfertigung des Stimmensatzes muß diese in der Partitur oft nur skizzierte Umgestaltung weiter vorangetrieben worden sein. Es handelte sich hierbei vor allem um die Ergänzung von Füllstimmen, Beseitigung überflüssiger Oktavverdopplungen, Übergang zu scheinpolyphoner Stimmführung sowie Zusatz von Vortragsbezeichnungen, Verzierungen und Durchgangsnoten. Das Aufführungsmaterial mit der definitiven Fassung des Konzertes ist leider verlorengegangen, so daß auf spätere Abschriften zurückgegriffen werden muß und die Authentizität der zahlreichen Abweichungen sorgfältiger Prüfung bedarf. Nähere Einzelheiten hierzu liefern Vorwort und Revisionsbericht unserer Partiturausgabe (EP 9384).

Hans-Joachim Schulze

Postface

Today Bach's harpsichord concertos (BWV 1052-1058) are regarded, without exception, as transcriptions of earlier works, most of which are now lost but which generally called for a violin as solo instrument. Nothing is known of his reasons for transcribing them for keyboard, but the physical features of the autograph score, fortunately still preserved in the Berlin Staatsbibliothek (*Ms. ms. autogr. Bach P 234*, collective manuscript with seven harpsichord concertos), point to the late 1730s as their date of origin. This suggests that they arose in connection with the Leipzig Collegium Musicum, whose directorship Bach had resumed in September 1739 after an interval of nearly two years. Whether the solo parts were taken by Bach himself or by one of his sons or pupils is a matter of speculation, as is the manner in which they were received by his contemporaries. It appears, however, that the D minor Concerto BWV 1052 soon acquired the status of a favorite.

This is clearly shown by the number and quality of the extant manuscript copies. It is highly probable that the concerto was revived in Berlin beginning some time around 1750, and another performance took place at the Berlin Singakademie in 1807 during the early years of the nineteenth-century Bach revival. The legacy of this tradition passed to Felix Mendelssohn Bartholdy, who incorporated the work in his repertoire no later than 1835. It was probably Mendelssohn's performance at the Leipzig Gewandhaus on 9 March 1837 that caused this "highly celebrated concerto" (Robert Schumann) to become the very first orchestral work by Bach to appear in print. The first edition, brought out in full score by Friedrich Kistner in Leipzig (1838), was followed by new editions based on a wider selection of sources, published 1854 by C. F. Peters and 1869 in volume 17 of the Bach Society Edition.

Nonetheless, Bach scholars have for some time expressed doubts regarding the authenticity of this piece. Not even the early reference to a lost violin concerto as the basis of Bach's transcription could lay these doubts to rest. Nor can the question of authenticity be separated from the convoluted origins of this work, which has come down to us in several conflicting versions. At present, the concerto's genesis presents itself as follows: All extant versions seem to derive from a violin concerto in D minor which, though lost, can be reconstructed with sufficient reliability. There is some question whether the thematic material, the violin writing, and the unequal handling of the contrapuntal parts warrant our speaking of the reconstructed concerto as a creation of J. S. Bach in every respect. The piece more likely dates from Bach's final years in Weimar (1714-17) than from the masterly period that followed in Cöthen.

The earliest evidence of Bach's arrangement of this violin concerto is found in two church cantatas, nos. 146 and 188. Cantata 146 only permits a hypothetical date of origin, while Cantata 188 can be fairly safely assumed to date from 1729. Both cantatas adopt a fast movement from the violin concerto as an introduction, scored for organ, strings, and woodwind. Cantata 146 also presents the slow movement in a bold reworking for four-part chorus. This strongly suggests that both cantatas originated at roughly the same time. Roughly between 1732 and 1734 Carl Philipp Emanuel Bach prepared a transcription in parts for harpsichord and strings (BWV 1052a), possibly for a performance by his father's Collegium Musicum.

Towards the end of the 1730s J. S. Bach, as already mentioned, produced his own arrangement. The string parts were only lightly touched up, but in order to adapt the solo part to the idiosyncrasies of the keyboard Bach made a great variety of changes to the solo violin part, now recast as a melody line for harpsichord, and to the continuo part, from which the bass line of the harpsichord was largely extracted. These alterations were often only sketched in the score and must have been worked out in greater detail in the set of parts. They primarily involved the adding of filler parts, the removal of extraneous octave doublings, a transition to pseudo-contrapuntal partwriting, and the addition of expression marks, ornaments, and passing notes. Unfortunately the performance material with the definitive version of the concerto is lost, and we are forced to rely on later manuscript copies and carefully to weigh the authenticity of the many deviations. Further information on this matter can be found in the preface and editorial notes in our edition of the full score (EP 9384).

Hans-Joachim Schulze